British Library Cataloguing
in Publication Data
Stobbs, William
The grape that ran away.
I. Title
823'.9'1J   PZ7.S/
ISBN 0-370-30255-9

Copyright © William Stobbs 1980
Printed and bound in Great Britain for
The Bodley Head, 9 Bow Street, London WC2E 7AL
by William Clowes (Beccles) Ltd
First published 1980

for Jessamy

a picture book by WILLIAM STOBBS

The Grape that Ran Away

THE BODLEY HEAD
LONDON SYDNEY
TORONTO

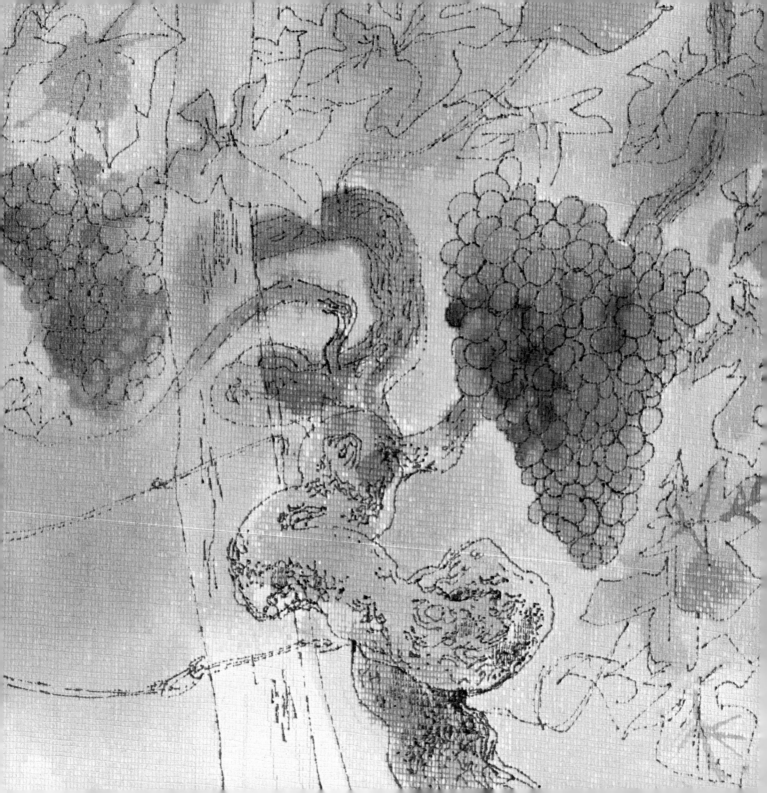

Long ago when animals and plants could speak, a
little grape was getting bored.

"Why should I stay here, elbowed by all these
other grapes?" she said to herself. "There must
be more to life than grapes. I will run away and
find out."

So she edged herself free, dropped to the ground,
and ran away.

But the vine on which the grape had been
growing saw her go.

"Help, help," she called.   "A little grape is
running away.   Catch her."

A butterfly who was fluttering by, taking
life easy as butterflies do, heard Mother Vine,
so she joined in.

"Help, help, a little grape is running away.
Stop her!"

A sparrow was perching on a branch nearby. He had seen the butterfly and he wanted to catch her and eat her for breakfast. He was not thinking about her beautiful colours, just the delicate taste. He, too, heard Mother Vine, so he joined in.

"Help, help! A little grape is running away. Stop her!"

But he was going to eat the butterfly just the same.

High above, a sparrow hawk soared. Just as the sparrow wanted the butterfly for breakfast, so did the hawk want the sparrow. He swooped down. Then he heard them all calling out, "Help, help! A little grape is running away. Stop her!"

So he joined in, and Mother Vine, the butterfly, the sparrow and the sparrow hawk were all shouting, "Help, help! A little grape is running away. Stop her!"

A huge cloud floated by, and saw the coming
and going of all four of them. So he joined in,
with his thunder voice.

"Stop, little grape, and at once. Go back
to the vine."

But the grape kept running.

   In a rage, the thunder cloud took careful aim and launched a bolt of lightning which would stop all this nonsense, but he missed. The lightning and torrents of rain fell in a brook full of tadpoles, and having heard the voice of the thunder, they all squeaked.

   "Stop, little grape, and at once.   Stop, little grape, and at once!"

Soon the tadpoles were being chased by a sunfish
who wanted them for breakfast, so he joined in,
"Stop, little grape, and at once."

In the sky, the sparrow hawk, the sparrow, and
the butterfly were all shouting.

"Help, help, a little grape is running away.   Stop
her!"

Where the brook ran into a wider stream, a rainbow trout was swimming. Beautiful, but hungry, he saw the sunfish.

"What a good lunch she would make," he said. Then he heard the sunfish singing and the tadpoles squeaking, "Stop, little grape, and at once."

"What nonsense," said the trout, and took a bite at the sunfish's tail. He missed. But he joined in the procession, singing in his trout voice, "Stop, little grape, and at once."

The stream now merged with the big river and a
huge pike came along.

"What a splendid dinner," he said. "Three
courses. Tadpoles, sunfish and trout. What an
absurd song they are singing; absolute nonsense,
but I will join in until I have eaten them all up."

"Stop, little grape, and at once," he sang in his
deep, deep, deep pike voice.

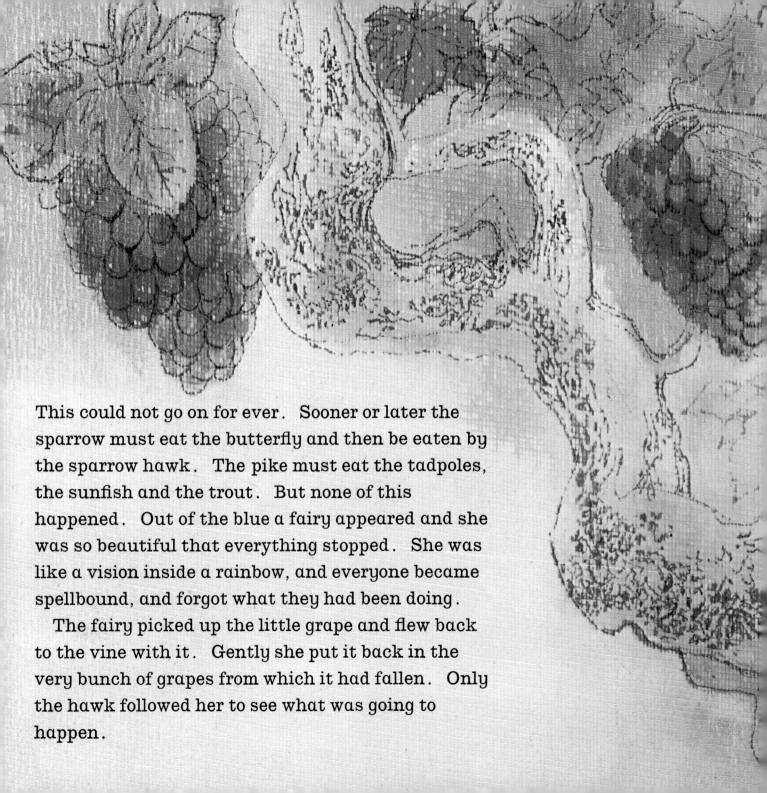

This could not go on for ever. Sooner or later the sparrow must eat the butterfly and then be eaten by the sparrow hawk. The pike must eat the tadpoles, the sunfish and the trout. But none of this happened. Out of the blue a fairy appeared and she was so beautiful that everything stopped. She was like a vision inside a rainbow, and everyone became spellbound, and forgot what they had been doing.

The fairy picked up the little grape and flew back to the vine with it. Gently she put it back in the very bunch of grapes from which it had fallen. Only the hawk followed her to see what was going to happen.

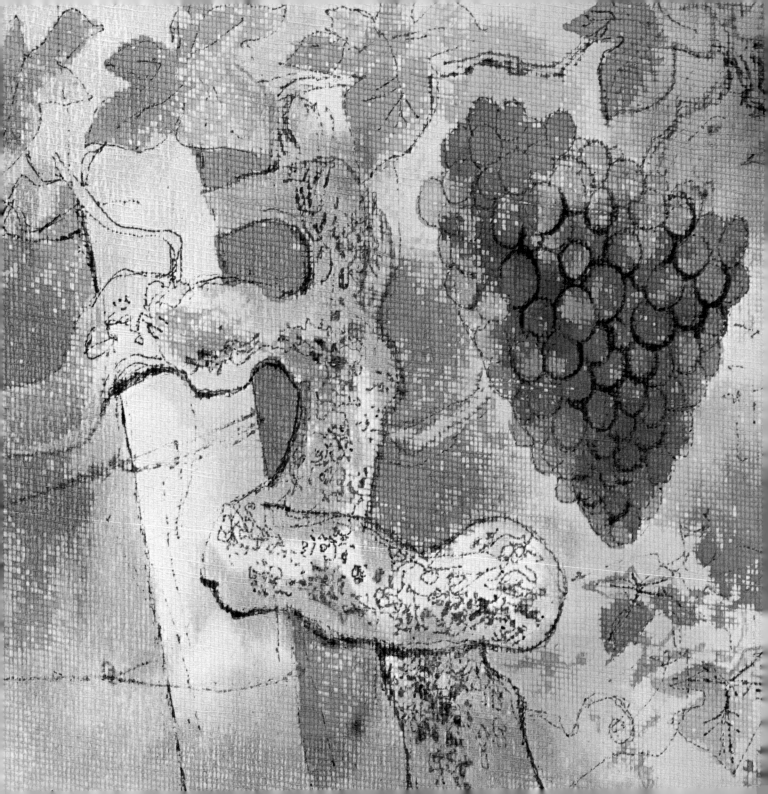

When the little grape was safely settled in the bunch, she boasted about her adventure for days.

The sun shone hot and strong through July and August, and in September, when the pickers came to pick the grapes to make wine, one bunch did not go off with the wine harvest.

That special bunch with the
runaway grape in it was eaten.
    And I know who ate it.
    It was you.
    You who are reading this story!